Phonics Focus: vowel + r (er)

THE NERDS

BY CHRISTINA EARLEY

ILLUSTRATED BY
BELLA RECH

A Blue Marlin Book

Introduction:

Phonics is the relationship between letters and sounds. It is the foundation for reading words, or decoding. A phonogram is a letter or group of letters that represents a sound. Students who practice phonics and sight words become fluent word readers. Having word fluency allows students to build their comprehension skills and become skilled and confident readers.

Activities:

BEFORE READING

Use your finger to underline the key phonogram in each word in the *Words to Read* list on page 3. Then, read the word. For longer words, look for ways to break the word into smaller parts (double letters, word I know, ending, etc.).

DURING READING

Use sticky notes to annotate for understanding. Write questions, make connections, summarize each page after it is read, or draw an emoji that describes how you felt about different parts.

AFTER READING

Share and discuss your sticky notes with an adult or peer who also read the story.

Key Word/Phonogram: n**er**d

Words to Read:

her	headers	soccer
herd	Jasper	summer
nerd	jersey	super
nerves	laser	superb
served	layer	tigers
alert	maker	timer
Amber	matters	towers
batter	member	ulcer
brother	mixer	walker
butter	monster	winner
center	mother	winter
Chandler	number	bakery
Chester	observes	buttercream
clever	Peter	camera
derby	Piper	defender
exerts	player	energy
experts	power	entering
farmer	prefers	interest
father	river	silvery
flower	shelter	together
gamer	sister	

Meet the Nerd family. Each family member has a special interest.

This makes them super experts on these matters.

Sister Piper is a nature nerd. She uses her camera to keep track of what she observes.

One summer, she saw a herd of elk near a flower bed next to the silvery river.

She is a dog walker at the Chandler Animal Shelter.

Brother Peter is a soccer nerd. He is a player on the Chester Tigers. His jersey number is five.

As a center back, he is a defender. His headers stop balls from entering the goal.

He exerts a lot of energy in each game.

Mother Amber is a bakery nerd. She puts butter in the mixer to make her superb cake batter. As the maker of layer cakes, she uses lots of buttercream.

One of her cakes was served at a winter wedding for a farmer. It had nine towers! While stacking it, her nerves almost gave her an ulcer.

Father Jasper is a gamer nerd. He prefers laser and monster video games.

He was clever and alert in last year's Power Derby. When the timer went off, he was the winner. The Nerd family celebrated together.

Quiz:

1. **True or false?** The sister is a bakery nerd.
2. **True or false?** The farmer's wedding cake was nine towers high.
3. **True or false?** Peter is the goalie on his soccer team.
4. What does the story tell you about what it means to be a nerd?
5. Why did Jasper win the Power Derby?

Flip the book around for answers!

Answers:
1. False
2. True
3. False
4. Possible answer: Being a nerd means that a person is an expert on something.
5. Possible answer: He was alert and clever.

Activities:

1. Write a story about something that you are an expert on.

2. Write a new story using some or all of the "er" words from this book.

3. Create a vocabulary word map for a word that was new to you. Write the word in the middle of a paper. Surround it with a definition, illustration, sentence, and other words related to the vocabulary word.

4. Create a meme about the "er" key word "nerd."

5. Design a game to practice reading and spelling words with "er."

Written by: Christina Earley
Illustrated by: Bella Rech
Design by: Rhea Magaro-Wallace
Editor: Kim Thompson
Educational Consultant: Marie Lemke, M.Ed.
Series Development: James Earley

Library of Congress PCN Data
The Nerds (er) / Christina Earley
Blue Marlin Readers
ISBN 979-8-8873-5297-8 (hard cover)
ISBN 979-8-8873-5382-1 (paperback)
ISBN 979-8-8873-5467-5 (EPUB)
ISBN 979-8-8873-5552-8 (eBook)
Library of Congress Control Number: 2022951090

Printed in the United States of America.

Seahorse Publishing Company
seahorsepub.com

Copyright © 2024 **SEAHORSE PUBLISHING COMPANY**

All rights reserved. No part of this publication may be reproduced, stored in a retrieval system or be transmitted in any form or by any means, electronic, mechanical, photocopying, recording, or otherwise, without the prior written permission of Seahorse Publishing Company.

Published in the United States
Seahorse Publishing
PO Box 771325
Coral Springs, FL 33077